# Compounding Wisdom

*A Young Person's Guide to Financial Success*

## Larry Jones

Copyright ©2017 Larry Jones

All rights reserved. No part of this book may be reproduced in any form without permission in writing from the publisher, except in the case of brief quotations embodied in critical articles or reviews.

All Scripture quotations, unless otherwise indicated, are taken from the Holy Bible, New International Version.

ISBN-13: 9781976182365

ISBN-10: 1976182360

Images courtesy of pixabay.com

NavStar Financial Services is a full service planning firm located in Mooresville, NC. Owned by Larry Jones, ChFC the firm specializes in comprehensive planning and investment advisory services, as well as advanced estate planning. Larry can be reached at 704 663-7482 or e-mail him at larry@navfs.com

*Investment advisory services offered through Horter Investment Management, LLC, a SEC-Registered Investment Advisor. Horter Investment Management does not provide legal or tax advice. Investment Advisor Representatives of Horter Investment Management may only conduct business with residents of the states and jurisdictions in which they are properly registered or exempt from registration requirements. Insurance and annuity products are sold separately through NavStar Financial Services. Securities transactions for Horter Investment Management clients are placed through Trust Company of America, TD Ameritrade and Jefferson National Life Insurance Company.*

In 1994 I was a struggling single parent of a three year old and over $20,000 in debt. I was unable to work at my profession, a professional yacht captain, had a limited formal education, and was working for not much more than minimum wage in a factory in Mooresville, NC.

Two things happened that year to change the course of my life. I accepted Christ, and I heard Larry Burkett on the radio.

Burkett was a Christian financial counselor who founded an organization called Christian Financial Concepts. Burkett had done an exhaustive study on everything the Bible had to say about money, and he became an advocate of using the Biblical concepts of handling money to order our personal finances. Everyday he would come on our local Christian radio station, and I hung on every word. I decided to follow the Lord's leading in this and began to put into practice the things that Burkett taught. He didn't disappoint me.

Before two years had passed I had gotten completely out of debt and was a student in college, where I received my degree in business in 1998. I'll forever be grateful to God and Larry Burkett.

Larry passed away in 2003. Since then a number of disciples of Burkett have gone on to become well-known financial counselors. It seems to me, however, that many of the principles that Burkett constantly preached are unknown to the next generation. It's my hope that this book will revive those amazing truths that never grow old, and that they will bless someone else as much as they have me.

I'd like to dedicate this book to him, and ultimately to the One who transformed both Larry Burkett and me, the Lord Jesus Christ.

To Him be the glory.

# Contents

Introduction        6

Don't Plan to Fail        9

You're Going to Need Some Money        21

If You Aim at Nothing You'll Hit it Every Time        30

The Captain is on the Bridge        38

Who Are You Working For, Anyway?        45

Slavery is Illegal...Isn't It?        52

There IS a Free Lunch (well, sort of)        60

What Could Possibly Go Wrong?        66

Giving to Caesar        72

The Key to Happiness        79

Let's Make a Run for It        84

Touchdown!        86

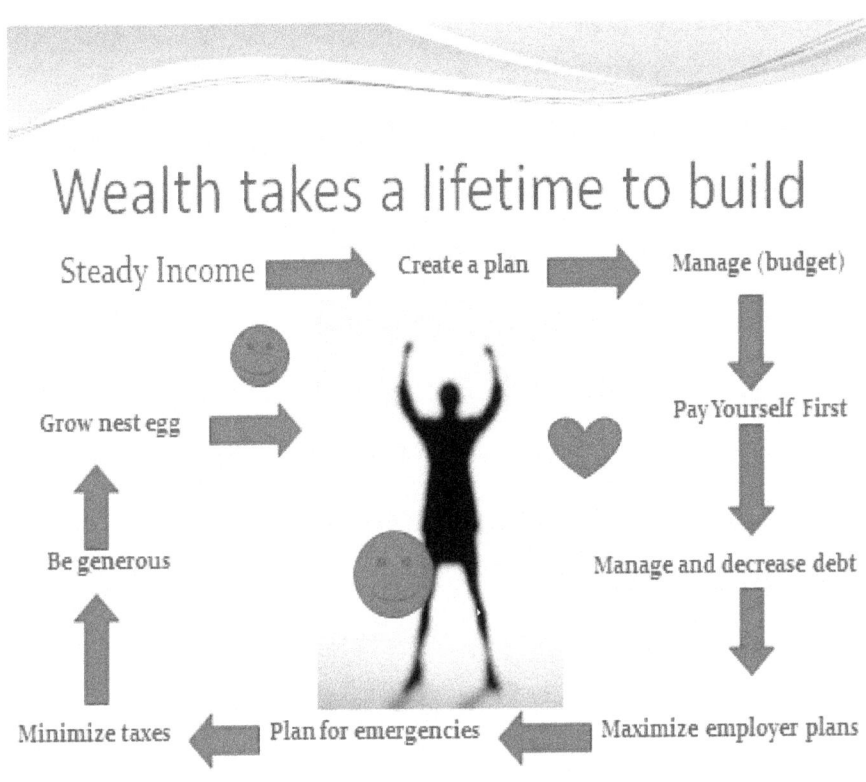

**Are You Ready to Begin Your Journey to Financial Freedom?**

# Introduction

The road to wealth isn't an interstate highway. If it were almost everyone would end up there. It's more like the famous contest between the Tortoise and the Hare. Guess who won that contest? We all remember that the lowly turtle, by plodding deliberately along, taught the bunny a lesson never to be forgotten. What was that lesson? Keep at it and you'll succeed. When it comes to your financial life, the same lesson holds true.

As an observer of financial things, I never cease to be amazed at some of the bad financial decisions that folks make along the path of life. I've made some of them myself. Why does one person end up on easy street while another has to sweep it?

Well, it's quite simple, really. During the course of our lives we all make decisions along the way, which will have a major impact on our future. Now, I'll grant that some start out with advantages that others don't have, but that's no matter. I still believe that in this great free enterprise system, which we call the United States of America, certain decisions will cause certain results, certainly. Anyone, with grit and determination, not afraid to work hard, and making sound decisions using the wisdom that God gave, can and will succeed.

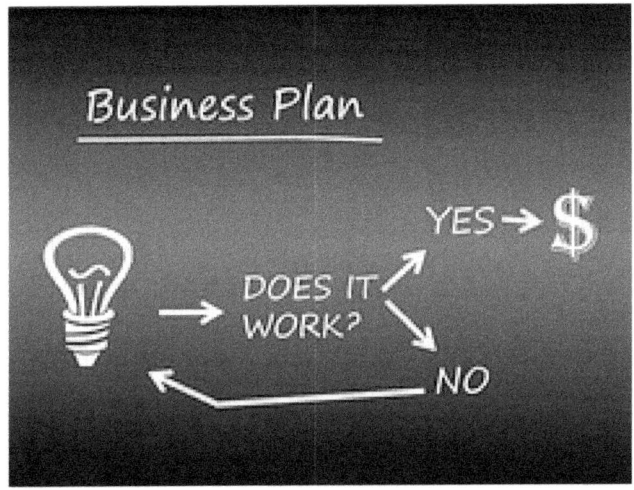

**The question is: are you willing to walk this road? Many are not.**

My name is Larry Jones, and I am a financial planner. I have spent a great deal of time learning and analyzing advanced financial concepts. I can tell you about intentionally defective grantor trusts and explain beta and tax strategies. This book isn't about those things. This book is designed to give the non-financial person the tools he or she needs to reach total financial independence.

Wouldn't it be nice if you had a roadmap? A set of defined, and easy steps, that you could order your financial life by? Even better, how about something that you don't have to acquire an MBA to understand? If that sounds good, then this book was written for you.

I hope you enjoy reading it as much as I did writing it!

# Chapter 1

# Don't Plan to Fail
*(by failing to plan)*

Have you been to any of your favorite restaurants, only to find the doors locked, and a permanent "Closed" sign hanging? Have you known anyone who had a serious illness that sent the family finances into the red? Have you ever heard of a congressional representative signing a bill into law without reading it beforehand (Sorry...I couldn't resist)? Of course you have, and all of these events would serve as a good example of what happens when you ignore our first Biblical financial principle: **Plan for the future.**

We all plan for our future, at some level. The young person who works hard in school, does his homework, gets a job as a teenager, and then goes on to college, and even postgraduate school isn't doing that because he enjoys hitting the books. No, he knows that some suffering in the short term will pay off in the long term. He is planning for the future.

The Bible would call him wise.

**Proverbs 21:5**

*The plans of the diligent lead surely to advantage, But everyone who is hasty comes surely to poverty.* (Topical Bible)

I have had folks say to me, "I just live by faith! I don't make any plans for my future, because I know the Lord will take care of me." Well, it's true. He will. The Bible has no end of praise for those who have great faith, but He has also given you a brain, and faith consists of believing what God says. The Bible clearly tells us to plan how we should live and prosper.

If you would like to test the wisdom of this precept, ask any retiree who spends most of their free time worrying about how they will meet their financial obligations. I speak with many individuals who have worked their whole lives without putting anything away. At some point, health and the ability to earn income will subside. That's why it's important to put together a plan when you are young.

How do you construct a plan? Here are some step-by-step guidelines, which if followed over a lifetime, will lead to financial security.

Guaranteed.

> *Proverbs 13:16*
> *A wise man thinks ahead; a*
> *fool doesn't, and even brags*
> *about it! (Living Bible)*

*Luke 14:28-30*
"Suppose one of you wants to build a tower. Won't you first sit down and estimate the cost to see if you have enough money to complete it? For if you lay the foundation and are not able to finish it, everyone who sees it will ridicule you, saying, 'This person began to build and wasn't able to finish.'"

# Step 1: Get a Job!

If you intend to build a financial dynasty for yourself, you are going to need some way to fund it. The only way I know to support that goal over the long haul is to get a job. Then stick to it! You must protect that job at all costs, until you can find a better job.

If an education will allow you to earn a better living, then by all means, educate yourself. Take advantage of any opportunity to improve your position. Husbands and wives can become a great team in this regard. For example, take the situation of a young couple right out of high school. Both spouses have low paying jobs, and no secondary education. If they work as a team, they can get on a budget, pay off debt, and then one spouse can stop working, or work part time to go back to college.

Sure, it might be tough. But when that first spouse graduates, their family income should rise. At that point, the first spouse goes to work, and the other one goes back to school. In this way, over a few years, a family income can rise substantially!

But remember, divorce nullifies all financial plans.

## Step 2: Create a Plan

Now that you have a steady income, it's time to start thinking about where you would like to end up financially. Visualize for yourself what your ideal retirement life will look like, and then put together a financial plan for yourself to get there. Life is hard, and situations change, so be ready to adapt your plan to reality, from time to time. If it helps to enlist the aid of a financial professional, then by all means do it. If his or her advice is sound it will be money well spent.

## Step 3: Manage Your Plan

A financial plan will necessarily change over time. How do you know how you're doing? You don't unless you have some sort of budget to live by. You need to know where your money is going. A budget is the only tool that will constantly tell you that.

How will you grow your money? What is your tolerance for risk? Should you be in the stock market? Or are there other alternatives for investment? How will children change your plans (they will!) ? What about taxes? What if you die prematurely? Etc....a good financial plan should be actively managed to deal with all of these contingencies.

## Step 4: Pay Yourself First

Who are you working for anyway? Certainly not for Duke Energy or Uncle Sam. One of the reasons that Communism has never worked is because people just will not work very hard to support someone else. It's human nature. With that being said, I would suggest that any week you work and don't save anything for yourself is a wasted week. No matter how much or how little you bring home, put something away for YOU. One day you'll have a pleasant surprise. If you only save $10 a week for your working years you'll have over $100,000 when you retire!

## Step 5: Manage, decrease, and eliminate debt

There is no more important principle than this one. Debt is a killer of the family budget, as well as a destroyer of happy homes!

Now, I realize that some debt is unavoidable. Not many young people have the cash available to buy a home outright, but maybe you can do without that Corvette and drive an $8000 Honda instead. Our parents knew how to do without if they couldn't pay for something. That's the reason they had money to leave to us, and that's also the reason that a lot of folks from my generation have nothing to leave to their children....

lifelong debt that robs the family treasury. The sooner you can get out of debt, the sooner you can really begin to put money away toward your own future. Before you do that you're just spinning your wheels.

## Step 6: Maximize Employer Plans

If your employer administers any type of retirement plan, such as a 401-K, where he offers to match any money that you contribute, you should do it to the greatest extent he allows. There is no faster way to accumulate a nest egg. If you are self-employed, you should look into setting up some type of tax-deferred savings vehicle for yourself.

## Step 7: Plan for Emergencies

In this life we are going to have unexpected emergencies and we'd better be prepared for them (to be prepared for the next life, I'd recommend reading the book of John).

That's the purpose of risk management, i.e. a good insurance plan. Health insurance, disability insurance, life insurance, homeowners and auto, and long-term care insurance all have a place in any well thought out financial plan.

Don't allow something that you could have foreseen to wreck your plan. I'd also recommend that you keep an emergency fund of cash on hand at all times. This fund should be able to pay all of your expenses for at least 6 months should you lose your income for any reason. A year is even better.

## Step 8: Minimize Taxes

When the income tax was originally signed into law the tax rate was less than 3%, and lawmakers argued that it would never exceed 5. The Revolutionary war was fought over less than a 3% tax, and the evil tax collectors in the Bible exacted about 10%!

Wouldn't you like to be able to keep 90% of what you make? Don't get me wrong, the Bible tells us to pay our taxes, and it's our civic duty to do so. But there are ways to legally decrease the amounts that you, and your heirs will have to pay to Uncle Sam. Don't overlook this easy way to increase what you take home to your family, and your nest egg.

## Step 9: Be Generous

This next step surprises a lot of people. But as long as we're thinking Biblically, you should know that I have never seen a stingy person end up happy and financially secure. God has a special place in His heart for the poor, and He will bless us if we will but bless others with what He has given us. He cannot fill a hand that is tightly clenched.

## Step 10: Grow Your Nest Egg

Ok, now you are out of debt, are being generous, have kept more of your income by paying less in taxes, and have contingency plans in place in case of emergencies. It's time to go for it!

Funnel as much as you can into your nest egg, and watch it grow exponentially.

## Step 11: Cross That Finish Line

Sooner than you think, the day of retirement will come upon you. If you have lived a lifetime of good financial planning, the rest will be easy (at least financially).

Well, what if you haven't been doing these things since you were young? Is it too late? No! Absolutely not. Of course, beginning younger is better, but it's never too late to get a plan together and get going. Harland Sanders was 80 years old when he started Kentucky Fried Chicken.

**So that's it....**

That's our roadmap in a nutshell. The next chapters will expound on this framework. So...are you ready?

Let's get started on our path to financial freedom!

*If you will do the things that you need to do when you are young, then you will be able to do the things you want to do when you get old!*

## Chapter 2

# You're Going to Need Some Money!

This is the keystone of your financial plan. Without an income nothing else can happen. In order to put an effective financial plan in place, you must have a regular opportunity to fund that plan. And it stands to reason that the better income you have, the better chance you'll have to reach your financial goals.

This is the very reason why our parents were so anxious to see us do well in school. They knew that education was the thing that would open doors to opportunity. Now, I know that someone like Billy Joel or George Clooney would say that a good education isn't necessary to succeed in life, and if you are a young music prodigy, or the most attractive person in your state that may be true, but for the vast majority of folks, a good education is going to be the difference between making $30,000 a year and making $130,000. Will you be any smarter with a college degree? Perhaps not, but there are some doors that will remain closed to you no matter how smart you are if you don't have one.

**Proverbs 6:6-8**
Go to the ant, you sluggard; consider its ways
and be wise!
It has no commander,
no overseer or ruler,
yet it stores its provisions in summer and
gathers its food at harvest.

We all remember the partiers in school, and the ones who later went on to become Doctors and Architects. Chances are they weren't the same people. Those who were wise recognized that God had endowed them with a good mind, and they saw opportunity in going to school. They made a decision early in life to discipline themselves and work hard. They kept their eye on the prize and it paid off for them.

"Well, Larry," you might say, "I was a partier." Or, "I'm a divorced single parent. Should I just give up? Is it too late for me?"

The answer is no. I was a 37 year-old single parent of a 5 year old when I went back to college. It can be done. You just have to have a "want to" that's strong enough. Wisdom is wise at whatever age you decide to apply it. Would you like to have a chance at an education? You can do it if you want to badly enough.

There are many sources of assistance if you choose this path. For me it was student loans. Yes, I had to pay them back, but knowing that I would be on the hook for that money was a strong incentive to graduate. Student loans are readily available today, as well as grants and scholarships. Perhaps you could find a way to work part-time while you went to school. Again...it's all up to you. I still believe that in America, you are only limited by yourself in what you can achieve.

## Are you married? You Can Work as a Team!

**A married couple has a huge advantage in bringing themselves up economically, if they will only stick together as a team.**

For example, take the young couple with no children (or maybe with) who only have a high school education. The wife works at a retail store and the husband is in construction. What would happen if the couple put together a budget based on the husband's income alone?

This would allow the wife to quit her job, and go back to school. Using student loans, or paying as she goes, she could begin at a low cost community college, and then finish up at a state university, of course pursuing a degree in something marketable. Once she graduated, she could then support her husband while he quit his job and went back to school. In this way the couple could raise themselves up financially.

Would it be hard? Yes! Could it be done? Absolutely yes! But keep in mind that this will only work with a very committed couple. A divorce will throw the entire plan onto the trash heap.

I realize that college isn't for everybody, but education isn't limited to college. Many trades offer exclusive certifications and specialties that will raise income levels. To me, one of the worst tragedies is working in a job that you hate all of your life. Try to find a career you'll enjoy.

In my opinion, one of the greatest failures in public school is the inability to point young people in a direction that they are gifted by God to go in. What do I mean by that?

The Bible clearly teaches that God gives different gifts to different people.... different likes and urges, etc.

For example I have a great love for the ocean and being at sea. Not many share that urge. That is something that God has put into me. I also enjoy business and finance. When I speak on financial topics I get excited. It might put you to sleep.

Different strokes for different folks. The key to being happy in your chosen career is in finding those particular gifts and longings that best fit your work in life. I believe that God has gifted each of us in a unique way, and it's one of His greatest gifts! He wants us to enjoy what we do for a living.

If you can do that you will always look forward to showing up on Monday morning. One of the best tools for uncovering those gifts that I have found is administered by an organization called Crown Ministries (founded by Larry Burkett). They have a process called "Career Direct" online. The cost is $80 and is one of the best services out there.

In this service you'll take an assessment test that will help show you where you are gifted along with suggestions about possible career paths. Many other resources are available, such as resume builders and career descriptions. It's the best $80 you'll spend. (FYI I took this assessment years ago, and made a career change because of it. It was one of the best moves I ever made.)

The link for this service can be found at:

https://secure.careerdirectonline.org/get/

My advice is to do everything you can to (1) secure a stable and reliable income, no matter the amount, and (2) maximize that income for as long as you can. Prepare yourself to enter into a job that you love, and then work at it with all your heart.

With that in place, you'll be ready for step 2: **Create a plan**

So what are you waiting for? The world is waiting for you to say, "here I come. Try and stop me."

## Chapter 3

# If You Aim at Nothing, You'll Hit it Every Time

In the last chapter I covered the importance of having a steady income when it comes to reaching your retirement goals. It goes without saying that the person who swings from one job to another will not get the same results as the person who keeps the same job for 35 to 40 years.

In this chapter I want to take a look at the second step in achieving your financial dreams: having a plan.

**Proverbs 27:23**
Be sure you know the condition of your
flocks, give careful attention to your herds;

Let's face it, if you aim at nothing you will hit it every time! And when it comes to finances, that's what a lot of people do. Once you have that income, what do you do next?

It's time to do a top-down view of what you'd like your retirement to look like. Then you set your goals accordingly. Don't start with finances.

What?!!

"I thought this was a financial book, Larry! How can you say, 'picture your retirement, but don't start with finances'"?

Your finances are simply a means to an end. In other words, rather than focusing on how much money you'll need after you stop working, spend some time considering what you'll do after you retire? What kind of lifestyle would you like to have?

Will you go sailing around the world, or sit on the couch and watch Oprah all day? The second option, for me, might lead to an eventual suicide attempt, but it may work just fine for you. The point, is to picture what will make you happy. Keep in mind, too, that as you grow older these goals and priorities will quite likely change. Other events, such as getting married and having children will affect your picture as well.

Once you have gotten a picture of how you want to live, then it's time to try to calculate what kind of funds will be needed to pay for that lifestyle.

There are a couple of obstacles to overcome when planning for such a long time horizon:

## Inflation

What's inflation? It's simply the erosion of purchasing power over time. The easiest way to understand it is to remember the candy bar that you paid 25 cents for when you were a child. Now it costs $1.65 ! That's inflation. When prices go up, and income lags behind, then your ability to buy things has decreased. Inflation is particularly unkind to the average retiree, who may be living on a fixed income.

Economists tell us that inflation is caused by too much money in the nation's money supply chasing too few goods. Prices go up and inflation occurs. Now, with this country's policy of printing massive amounts of money, and injecting it into the economy, do you think inflation should be taken into account? Of course it should.

What kind or inflation rate should we assume, especially over a 30-40 year time period? In the late 70's the inflation rate was cruising along at the 12-14% level. Can we expect that level of inflation in the future? I certainly hope not, but I do believe that at some point, thanks to our government's monetary policies over the last eight years, we will most certainly see some significant rise in our inflation rates.

I do not, however expect high rates to last forever, and by averaging out the next 35 or so years, the plan can probably be done using an average 3% rate of inflation. Just remember that your plan should be revisited annually to see how you're doing, and adjusted accordingly.

## You Don't Know What You Don't Know

Huh? Well, if you are a young person just starting out you have a lot of years and a lot of living between today and that magic day of retirement. Your income will likely vary a great deal during those years. You might start out making minimum wage at Wendys and end up as CEO of a major corporation. How does one plan for those kinds of income variations?

What if you spend your life going from one job to another? Some do, especially in this crazy economy that we live in today. During the course of your life you will experience many significant financial events such as getting married, buying a home (or two), having children, and maybe even being a caregiver for your parents. That's why it's important to review your financial plan frequently and make changes when necessary.

There are two primary methods for determining what amount of money you need at retirement, the **Replacement Ratio** method, and the **Expense** method.

The first method assumes that the standard of living enjoyed during the years just prior to retirement will be the determinant of that same standard during the first years of retirement. In general a 60-80% ratio is used, so if you averaged $80,000 a year in your last 5 years of working, you should make 80% of that when you retire, or $64,000 a year.

The second, the expense method merely focuses on the projected expenses that the retiree will have in the first year of retirement. Using either of these methods, inflation should be taken into account.

For example, suppose you know that today your income is $65,000 a year, and you'd like to replace 80% of that income when you retire, which will be in 15 years. Using a 3% rate of inflation, you'll need a little over $101,000 to maintain that same standard of living.

Which method is best? Planners have been debating this for a long time. I like the replacement method. It will usually give a higher standard of living during retirement, in my opinion, especially when your goal will always be to limit expenses as much as possible anyway.

> A recent survey of financial planners listed a ranking of retirement objectives in order of priority:
> 1. Maintaining preretirement standard of living
> 2. Maintaining economic self-sufficiency
> 3. Minimizing taxes
> 4. Retiring early
> 5. Adapting to noneconomic aspects of retirement
> 6. Passing on wealth to others
> 7. Improving lifestyle in retirement.
> 8. Caring for dependents

So...do you have a plan? If you don't you're missing the boat. Should you get help crafting your plan? If you can afford it, yes. Using a professional for assistance can end up paying for the costs of such advice many times over.

## 4 Chapter

# The Captain is on the Bridge

I can't tell you how many groups of people I address in a typical year, where I preach the virtues of having a defined and well thought out plan for reaching our financial goals. I'm always surprised at how many of them *don't have any goals,* much less a defined plan of how to reach those goals. Nearly all of these folks will wholeheartedly agree with me that this is something they need to do, yet when I run into them a year later they will still be "intending to do that one day."

**Proverbs 6:4**
"Don't put it off; do it now!
Don't rest until you do.
(Living Bible)

Procrastination is, in my opinion, one of the biggest impediments to achieving most goals in life, and finances are no different. We make up our minds that we should do something, just not today. And so we decide to wait until tomorrow, but we're not promised tomorrow. Tomorrow may never come. Never base your family's financial future on uncertainty. Put your mind into your plans, and then once you are happy with the plan, implement that plan. Don't put it off.

I dealt with the importance of creating a financial plan in the last chapter. In this one, we'll take a look at the practical implementation of that plan. We'll need a way to measure our progress along the way, in order to know how we're doing, and to know when corrections need to be made. Planners use a tool known as the cash flow statement, which is just a glorified name for a budget.

## The Dreaded Budget

"Oh no," you might say. "I don't need a budget." What you really mean is that you don't want one. The Bible says (*Proverbs 21:20 – In the House of the wise are stores of choice food and oil, but a foolish man devours all he has.*) we should spend less than we make. Without a budget, you'll never know how you are doing in that regard. It will only become clear when your credit card balances are maxed out, and a crisis situation has developed. When your income each month is unable to keep up with outgo you are in an unsustainable situation (somewhat reminiscent of our national budget, hmmm...), and some drastic changes will necessarily have to be made. At that point, you will have become an indentured servant to your creditors, and they will remind you on a monthly basis of who you really are working for.

What am I saying here? A budget is not a tool to make you a slave, but A TOOL TO SET YOU FREE! Everyone needs a budget.

Starting a budget involves two steps:

## Step 1: Determine your present level of spending

I usually advise that you keep a log of where and how you spend every penny each day for a month. At the end of the month you'll analyze that log. You'll usually be surprised at how much goes out on a daily basis for things you don't need. A critical skill in financial discipline involves distinguishing between your needs, wants, and desires, and then allocating your resources wisely. For example, I'd like to stop typing right now and fly to south Florida and purchase that 150 foot yacht I've always wanted. That decision is a definite want. It does not, however, fit my budget at this particular time, and so I'll just have to be happy watching the travel channel. Our goals need to be realistic.

After 30 days of collecting your spending data, you'll begin to get some idea of where your money goes, possibly for the first time. Once you realize that you're spending $1500 a year at Starbucks, it can be an eye-opener, and positive change can result.

When doing this, you should also identify your other expenses that you have each year that are not necessarily included in that monthly calculation that you just did.

For example, you might pay your property taxes each year. Annual expenses should be divided by 12, and then folded into that monthly budget. Suppose you pay $1200 once each year for property taxes. You'd divide that by 12 to get $100 each month, and that number needs to be included in your budget. In other words, you need to add $100 to save each month to pay those taxes at the end of the year. Every unusual and annual expense needs to be accounted for in this way.

By the time you finish this, you'll have a very accurate and clear picture of where your money is going.

# Step 2: Establish the Budget

What is the ideal budget? It's a tool that perfectly accounts for where your money comes from, where it goes, and how it should be allocated. Your monthly income should exactly match the amounts you have allocated to the categories of your budget. There should be no negative numbers in the ideal budget.

I like to break the budget into needs, wants and desires. Needs are just that. You must have these categories covered. Such items as housing, food, clothing, etc. are definite needs. Wants are about choices in quality. For example, I want a steak, but maybe a hamburger will do. A new car vs. a used car, etc. Desires are those things that you get out of surplus funds after the above obligations have been met.

What are some of the obstacles to living on a budget? In our materialistic world the pressure is enormous to break your budget. You deserve the best, baby! You only go around once in life. He who dies with the most toys...is still dead! We've all heard this stuff, and it's ingrained in us. If we get in trouble we'll get a "debt consolidation loan" and all will be back to normal. But the debt keeps piling up. The problems haven't been solved, only postponed.

Here are some sample categories that your budget could include, along with percentage allocations, for example, let's say your gross income is $60,000 each year. Your budget might be set up something like this:

**Gross Income: $60,000**
- **Tithe** ($6000)
- **Taxes** ($13,200)
= **Net Spendable Income**   $40,800 or ($3400 mo.)

| | | |
|---|---|---|
| **Housing** | (27%) | $918.00 |
| **Food** | (11%) | $374.00 |
| **Auto** | (12%) | $408.00 |
| **Insurance** | (5%) | $170.00 |
| **Debts** | (5%) | $170.00 |
| **Recreation** | (7%) | $238.00 |
| **Clothing** | (6%) | $204.00 |
| **Savings** | (5%) | $170.00 |
| **Medical** | (4%) | $136.00 |
| **Misc.** | (7%) | $238.00 |
| **Investments** | (11%) | $374.00 |

Keep in mind that this is what you can spend each month and no more. If you have other categories, or you need to allocate more to food, for example, it would have to be taken from another category.

Again, this is only one example of a working budget and yours might be entirely different, depending on where you are in life and where you want to go. Remember, a budget needs to be revised from time to time, for example, when you pay off all debt, then that would free up that category for something else, ideally for savings or investments.

There are lots of benefits to living on a budget. Any business owner knows that to survive, a budget will be required. It's no different for the individual.

**Creating and managing a budget takes commitment and discipline, but in the end it will <u>set you free.</u>**

With a steady income, a definite plan, and the budgetary tool set up, now it's time to have fun growing wealth.

We'll look at that in the next chapter.

## Chapter 5

# Who are you Working for, Anyway?

One of my clients told me once that when she was a child, her Father had told her, before she was to start at her first job, that if she would just remember two things she would be successful. Her told her to act as if the business that she would be working at was her very own, and to, no matter what, always put something from each paycheck away for a rainy day. What good advice that was!

**Romans 4:4**
"Now to the one who works, his wages are not counted as a gift but as an obligation"

The next two topics that we'll discuss are "Pay yourself first," and "Decrease debt," in that order. My parents grew up in the 1930's, in the midst of the great depression. There was no governmental safety-net to speak of during those years. You either worked, or you didn't eat, and the folks who lived through those years never forgot how it was. They developed a frame of mind that basically said, "let's not go into debt for anything." In other words, if you couldn't pay cash for it, you didn't get it. These same folks later went off to serve in World War II, and then returned to work hard, save their money, and build the greatest economy and season of prosperity the world had ever seen. They are aptly called they "greatest generation."

However something changed in the sixties. With the introduction of credit cards, debt became a commodity. It was in the interest's of the credit card companies to keep you in debt forever. For the first time lending institutions began to use the term "deadbeats" not to refer to those who didn't pay their debts, but to those who did!

It has become an insidious financial cancer that now taints everything we do, and I believe it is such a violation of Biblical principles, that it will eventually wreck entire economies. You simply cannot pay off debt with more debt, and keep it up forever.

The average college graduate today has no thought of waiting until he can afford something before he acquires it. He can get everything on credit. Even his college education! As a result, the young person gets paid each week, and then must sit down and write checks to pay off all of his creditors, to the extent that he's got nothing left for himself. We have reversed the last two financial goals.

The typical American today has very little in savings. It's not that he wants it that way, but that's how it works out. Many never come out from under this financial rock, and end up retiring with few personal savings and only Social Security to live on. I see it every day.

The typical loan repayment for a college graduate today is around $35,000. That doesn't include any other debt he may have. If he takes ten years to pay that back, his payments will be somewhere north of $350-400 a month. Now, let's suppose that instead of paying back a loan, that same young person had socked away $350 a month for himself for thirty years. Assuming an 8% return on his money (which, by the way, isn't unreasonable....even today), he would have nearly half a million dollars to add to his Social Security payments each month after retirement.

So which is better? Paying yourself, or paying back a loan? Duh!

Even if you only managed to save $10 a week for yourself, over thirty years time you would produce more than $60,000! The key is to methodically save, and let the time value of money work in your favor. The credit card companies understand this concept very well, and that's why they have thirty story buildings all over the country!

Why should you save for yourself? There are many good reasons: retirement, those emergencies that will inevitably come along as you walk through life, to have a cushion that will provide you peace of mind, etc. Once you have the other steps in place (a steady income, a plan, a budget...) then it's time to start building a hedge for yourself.

## The Emergency Fund

In 2008 many folks found out the importance of having a financial hedge, as millions of Americans were laid off, or had their hours cut back. It was more painful for those who had no cushion. You should have this safety net, and one of your priorities should be to put together an emergency fund.

How much should you put away in this fund? I'd recommend at least 6 months of your expenses, and a year's worth is even better. That way when bad things begin to happen you have some time to recover. An emergency fund may just save your family from extreme hardship. This fund should be laddered. What do I mean by that? Laddering is a strategy where you take advantage of whatever interest you could be earning while you are accessing your emergency fund. Let me give an example:

Let's say that your expenses each month are $5000. You'd like to have at least $30,000 in your emergency fund, enough for six months. Instead of putting the entire $30,000 in a checking or savings account, which earns next to nothing, you should take $5000 and put it into a six-month CD (presumably paying more than a checking account...I know, I know....the amounts that banks are paying is laughable, but bear with me), then the next month put another $5,000 into another six-month CD. Continue this for the next four months until you have all $30K in CD's, with each maturing in six months. At the end of the surrender period just roll it over into another six month CD. Now, should you have an emergency, you can access each individual CD that is maturing each month to pay your bills, and leave the rest alone to earn interest.

A six-month emergency fund is absolutely essential, and should be high priority. You should allow nothing to invade this money except a family-threatening financial earthquake. Buying those new Yosemite Sam mud flaps for your truck do not qualify as a reason to take money from this fund! Be ruthless.

Once your emergency fund is in place you have some wriggle room should you lose your job. The interview for your next position will go much smoother when you don't have the attitude of "if I don't get this job I'm sunk."

If you will implement these plans for growing wealth into your own situation, you will be miles ahead of 90% of the American public, and the emergency fund is a vital part of that plan.

Remember....PAY YOURSELF FIRST! When you reach over at dark-thirty each day to shut that alarm off, remember who you are getting out of bed for. Certainly not the credit card company or Uncle Sam (more on that later), but for you.

A week where you work and don't pay yourself is a wasted week.

In the next chapter we'll take a look at how the debt monster has wormed his way into every aspect of American life, how he eats away at your retirement lifestyle, and how to defeat him.

# Chapter 6

# Slavery is Illegal, isn't it?

My Father came up the hard way. He grew up in Ashe county NC, in the heart of Appalachia. His Father was a farmer and school teacher, presiding over grades 1 through 7 in a one-room schoolhouse. Well, my Dad was pretty good at Baseball. He was a pitcher, and in fact he was good enough to make it onto a triple-A minor league team in Kannapolis NC (that's where he met my Mom!). In the middle of the Great Depression, he was making $150 a month, a lot of money in those days, to play a game. He was just about to transition to the major leagues when the Japanese attacked Pearl Harbor. Instead of going to St. Louis to play ball, he found himself on a ship headed for WWII. He once told me that that was the maddest he'd ever been! I'll bet that's an understatement. His baseball career was over.

> **Proverbs 22:7**
> "The rich rule over the poor,
> And the borrower is slave to
> the lender."

He and my Mom got married in 1945, and having come through the Depression, knew what it was like to have a meal of pinto beans and cornbread, and to be grateful for it. The Greatest Generation always had a sense of gratitude. Neither of my parents had more than a High School education, though both were very smart. I doubt if my Dad ever made more than $250 a week in his entire life, yet when he passed away he owned two homes, one on Lake Norman, about 4 acres of land, a couple of cars, and had over $100,000 in the bank!

How did he do that?

He didn't believe in owing money to anybody. With the exception of a home mortgage, and some car payments in the early years, he paid cash for everything. Someone once told him that he needed a credit card or his credit rating would suffer. His response was, "why do I care about my credit rating?" Now that's freedom!

## Debt is a Killer!

Let's move ahead to 2015. Debt has now become a commodity. The average student leaves college with around $35,000 in student debt, with a monthly payment of around $400. That same student probably has, or soon will have a car payment, let's say $200 a month. Unless he or she wants to move back in with their parents, they'll be paying rent, or a mortgage somewhere between $700-900 a month. So far we're up to an immediate need after graduation for around $1400 a month, or almost $17,000 a year. AND THAT'S JUST TO PAY OFF LOANS!

He's behind the eight-ball before he ever get's hired by anyone. He's not free to find the best job for himself, but instead must immediately take what he can get. This graduate is going to need a starting salary of $35-40K to have any chance of success.

Next comes lovely little Sally...the girl of his dreams. They get married, buy a larger home, another car, a Biltmore House sized load of the finest Early American furniture, all on easy credit terms. After the 5th child, Sally begins to munch down $300 a week in groceries (which leads to major healthcare expenses down the road, but we'll address that in another chapter) and everyone lives happily ever after.

Especially the Visa and Mastercard Executives.

What are the odds that this couple will retire debt-free with two homes, and lots of retirement cash? What are the odds that they will even be together at all, after the financial strain takes it's toll?

It's not a pretty scenario, but it's the one that our culture, our media, and our impressive marketing machine is pitching them. There is a reason why Visa, American Express, and Bank of America have forty story buildings and you don't.

It's time to get a grip. It's time to grow up, and take a serious look at the benefits of delayed gratification. Albert Einstein said that the most powerful force in the Universe was compounding interest. He may be right.

Let's say you have a credit card that you owe $16,000 on and they are charging you 16% interest. Your payment will be around $300 a month. Believe it or not, many folks use this kind of thing as a revolving fund and some take as much as 20 YEARS to pay it off! If you do this you will have paid back over $72,000!

Now why would anyone want to start out with that kind of burden early in life? It just doesn't make sense. Think about it, anything this person earns in his investment portfolio that is less than 16% is losing him money! It's being wiped out by debt.

## The Starting Point

I have heard all the arguments about good debt and bad debt, and leveraging other people's money, etc. To a point I agree with some of these ideas. For example, it's not likely that the average person will be able to pay cash for a home, or perhaps even a car. But beyond that, I'd recommend limiting debt wherever possible. After all, the more of your money you can keep and invest the better off you'll be, in the long run. The goal is to live within your means. You shouldn't use borrowed money to pay for normal living expenses, and so the starting point is to not go into debt. If you are already feeling the pain of too much debt, it's time to get ruthless about getting rid of it. Here's a good way to do that.

## The Snowball Method

What I am going to describe next is one of the most impressive strategies for eliminating debt that I have ever seen. I first heard of this technique in 1994 from a Christian financial counselor named Larry Burkett. I personally used this method to slay over $20,000 worth of debt in a very short time, when I was a highly indebted single parent. Here's how it works.

Let's say I have the following debts:

There is a monthly payment of $50 a month on a VISA credit card with a balance of $1500, a payment of $75 a month on a Mastercard and a $2000 balance. There is also a $100 payment to the furniture store, where I owe $3000, along with a car payment of $250 a month, and a balance due of $6000.

My total payments on these debts are $475 a month, and a total balance of $12,500. If I make the minimum payments on these debts it will take me years to pay it off. But I'm not going to make the minimum payments.

I'll attack the easy one first. Every extra dime I can afford will go toward paying off that VISA card. Let's say I can pay this one off in 5 months. Now I have an extra $50 a month to spend, right? Wrong. I will now add that $50 to my Mastercard payment. By doing that I'll pay that one off much quicker, in about 18 months. Next I'll add those two amounts to pay off my next bill. And so on.

Before you know it, I'm making a monster payment each month toward paying these debts down. That's the snowball method and it will work for you too. As you watch these balances decline at greater and greater speed, you'll be greatly encouraged! You will be winning this battle against the debt monster, and it feels good. But the key is discipline.

You have to set goals and stick to them. It will mean denying yourself in the short term, but in the long run it will set you free. You must learn to see debt as the future-killer that it is.

OK....let's recap a bit. So far our plan to achieve financial freedom has included these steps: (1) get a job. A lifelong steady source of income is essential, (2) create a plan for yourself. If you aim at nothing you'll hit it every time, (3) get on a budget and manage that plan. Be determined about it, (4) always pay yourself first, and finally (5) eliminate debt wherever possible.

I wish I had known and followed these steps when I was a young person. If you have followed this advice then you are well on your way to financial freedom, and you are probably ahead of 90% of your peers. It's never too late to get started on this path, but of course, the more time you have to let your money grow the better off you'll be.

In the next chapter I'm going to talk about some free money that may be available to you.

# Chapter 7

# There is a Free Lunch
*(well, sort of)*

If I came up to you and said, "If you'll give me $1 I'll give you back $2," would you take that deal? All day long, right? How about if I added another carrot, and offered to let you defer paying the tax on that $1 you just made (yes, you have to pay the tax on it! Ask any game show winner.) until sometime in the future? Well, there's not much wrong with that deal, is there?

So why wouldn't you take that same deal from your employer?

**Proverbs 3:21**
"My son, do not let wisdom and understanding out of your sight, preserve sound judgment and discretion."

I once worked for a software company that would match our contribution to a 401(k) up to 8% of our income. What did that mean? If you made $80,000 a year, then you could contribute $6400 and the company would add another $6400! Now that's FREE MONEY!

I was speaking with one of my co-workers one day, and we got on the subject of our company sponsored 401(k). He told me that he had been working there for seven years and had never contributed a penny to it. Can you believe that? Imagine how much free money this fellow had missed out on in seven years. When I asked him why he didn't participate, his response was that he didn't want to "tie his money up." I guess doubling your money instantly didn't seem like a good idea to him.

This fellow was an engineer, but sometimes....you just can't fix stupid.

So far in our quest to achieve financial independence we have acquired a steady income, created a financial plan, implemented that plan and lived on a budget, we've made sure to pay ourselves first, and gotten out of debt as much as possible. We have a strong financial base set up. Now it's time to start growing our wealth. And one of the best ways to do that is to take advantage of our employer sponsored tax-deferred retirement plans.

## Tax-Deferred Retirement Plans

One of the ways that our wise benevolent Uncle Sam (tongue-in-cheek here) promotes growth in our economy, and also security for our elderly population, is through the tax code, which defines the rules for tax-advantaged savings vehicles, such as 401(k)'s and IRA's. These plans are designed to allow an employee to set aside a defined amount each year- there are set limits- which can then grow tax-free, at least for a while. Eventually our wise Uncle will require us to start paying the tax on earnings, but nevertheless, the ability to defer the payment of those taxes years into the future is powerful.

Let me give you an example:

Let's say you set aside $100 a pay period toward retirement. After thirty years you'd have over $218,000. But if you let it grow tax-deferred it would be worth more than $257,000. In my world 257 is more than 218.

There is a point to be made that it could be more complicated than that, of course. After all, you might be paying more taxes on that money later than you'd saved....and that's true, but still, remember that this is free money, if you are getting an employer match. My advice is to take as much advantage of this employer provided free money as possible, even if you do end up paying a lot of it back in taxes after retirement. Then consider supplementing this with a secondary retirement fund, owned by you, where you can minimize your tax consequences later on. A good financial planner (hint,hint) can help you do this.

One thing you need to do is to know how to calculate the maximum amounts that you should be contributing to get your employer match. There are limits defined by the IRS as to how much you can put in a 401(k) plan. In 2015 that limit was $18,000, but if you are 50 or older you are allowed to increase that amount to $24,000 each year.

And so, for example, your company tells you that they will match you up to 10% of your income. How much should you contribute? Here's how to figure that:

First, what is your income? If it's $100,000 a year, then they will match whatever you contribute up to $10,000 a year....in other words you'll be able to add $20,000 to your 401(k). But wait a minute. Isn't that more than the $18,000 limit allowed by the IRS? Yes, but here's the good part: your employer's money doesn't count against your $18,000 limit, although there is a combined limit of $53,000.

Now, keep in mind that your company won't match any more than that $10,000. Yet, you can still contribute more than that if you want to.

But should you?

In my opinion, probably not. Why not?

There are more efficient ways to accumulate your nest egg from a tax point of view. For example there are vehicles out there where you can earn around 7-8% year after year, with no market risk, and no taxes due upon withdrawal. These are better ways to grow wealth and keep it.

So why wouldn't you want to grow all of your assets this way?

Because you can't beat the free money that your employer is giving you. You should, however, not contribute more of your hard-earned money into the 401(k) than your employer will match.

The 401(k) with the employer match is a beautiful thing if your employer is generous. I have seen companies that offer a 401(k) but very little in matching contributions. If that's the case with you then maybe a good idea would be to set up your own IRA and fund it yourself. If you make it a Roth IRA then the growth is not taxed when you begin to withdraw the money. Also, if you are a small business owner there are tax deductions that you can take by funding certain retirement plans that you set up for yourself.

No matter what, make sure you are methodically paying yourself something each week. Don't forget who you're working for.

If you are following the strategies that I have outlined then you should be on a sound footing toward reaching the goal of financial independence.

Next, we're going to discuss protecting yourself against catastrophe.

# Chapter 8

# What Could Possibly Go Wrong?

Andy is a new college graduate who has been working at his firm for less than a year. He's on track with his financial plan. He's taking advantage of his employer's 401-K plan, and he also has a sweet little fiancé who he's anxious to start life with.

Before they are married he manages to tie up nearly all of his disposable income with credit card bills, payments on a new house, and furniture. Lots and lots of furniture. But that's OK. He has a nice salary.

On the Friday before his wedding, his company announces that they are cutting back, and since he's very junior with the firm, they'll be letting him go.

> **Job 14:1**
> "*Man, who is born of woman, is of few days, and full of trouble.*" (NKJV)

Audra is a single Mom with two small children, ages 3 and 5. Her husband made a good living, but now he's gone. He was killed in a car accident. Audra is a college graduate, but has been out of the workforce for over 5 years now. Her field was technology, and now the technology has passed her by. She has been looking for work, but finds that her choices are very limited because she needs to be available for her kids, and there are many opportunities that she just can't take advantage of. She is really struggling to keep everything together, and sometimes cries herself to sleep at night.

Bennie is a well known building contractor. He makes a good living, and his goal is to make a million dollars before he's 50. His job is highly physical, but he's in the best of shape. One day Bennie is balanced 3 stories up on a ladder, inspecting a gutter, when the ladder slips. Bennie lands on his back on concrete, and breaks his spinal chord. Now he's a paraplegic. Instead of working to hold his company together, he's learning how to do things like eat with a fork, and go to the bathroom without assistance. His whole world has changed, and the family wonders how they'll survive financially.

The names on the examples above have been made up, but the situations haven't been. These kind of things happen every day. Have you planned for them?

Have you ever known anyone who just seemed to have a dark cloud over their head, at least financially? No matter how they work and save to get ahead, something always seems to happen to wipe them out. Their car blows up, they get laid off, or they have a child in trouble who takes all their money. One thing that every human can count on is the fact that bad things are going to happen. It's life.

Now, if you've been following this post faithfully, and acting on these Biblical principles, you should have 300 employees of your own and be chauffeured around town by now. Well, maybe that's stretching it a little bit, but you should really be on very sound financial footing. As you grow your asset base, it's critical that you make plans for those emergencies that are going to come.

## Welcome to Armageddon!

I have an Attorney friend who tells me that in her world it's always Armageddon. Is she suicidal? No, what she means is that, as an Attorney she must always consider what the worst case is for any particular client, and protect them from that worst case. That's her job. When it comes to financial planning, that's not a bad philosophy. Risk management is all about planning for that Armageddon situation. So here's some practical steps to do just that:

**1) Build an emergency fund**

I recommend that everyone have at least a six month fund for emergencies. A year is even better. Make a list of all your financial obligations and start setting aside some money on a regular basis until you have that amount covered. I recommend laddering that money. This was covered in detail in chapter 5.

Imagine how much better all three of my examples above would have felt if they'd had this emergency fund.

**2) Move large risks to insurance companies.**

Life insurance will build an instant estate for you. If you have a family who depends on your income, and they'd be devastated financially by your absence, you <u>must remove that risk</u> by purchasing life insurance. Term life insurance can be had for pennies on the dollar, and transfers a huge risk to someone else.

Have you ever wondered what would happen if you took a month long unpaid vacation? What if it stretched to 3 months, or 6, or even longer? When you're disabled, that's what happens. Disability income insurance is an inexpensive way to protect yourself and your family from financial Armageddon.

How about health insurance? One stay in the hospital can cost you many thousands of dollars. Long term care insurance? End of life palliative care expenses can easily wipe out a boatload of assets. One rule of thumb I have on insurance is this: Ask the question, "If I didn't have this protection and the event happened, would it drastically alter my lifestyle? Would paying for this coverage drastically alter my lifestyle?" If the answer to the first question is yes, and the second one is no you should purchase the insurance.

In fact you are unwise not to.

## 3) Protect your assets from litigation

There are a number of things that you can do to protect yourself against being sued in todays litigious world. One easy solution is purchasing an umbrella insurance policy to protect your assets in the event of lawsuit. These policies are not expensive...a million dollars worth of liability coverage can be had for a few hundred dollars (or less) a year. Properly titling assets, and organizing your business in such a way as to maximize asset protection can also be critical.

**4) Manage the risk in your investment portfolio**

I can't tell you how many investors I've met with who have described themselves as "very conservative" yet when I examined their portfolio we discovered that their broker had put them in high to moderate risk funds. Usually they have no idea (although many of them are catching on after the start to 2016!). There's never any harm in getting a second opinion on your investments. It's important that the second opinion come from a Fiduciary. Ask your broker if they meet the Fiduciary level of standard. If they don't find another advisor.

Enacting these four steps will go a long way toward preventing major setbacks.

Now it's time to grow those assets!

## Chapter 9

# Giving to Caesar

At many of my seminars and classes I'll ask the question, "what is the largest item in your monthly budget?" The most common response is "the monthly mortgage payment", or perhaps the grocery bill. Those are all good valid answers but I feel fairly safe in declaring that for the vast majority of people, the biggest expense is..... are you ready for this?

taxes

That's right....taxes!

When I was a child it seemed that every politician campaigned on lowering taxes. In those days people liked to keep the money they went out and worked hard for each day. Not anymore. We actually have Presidential candidates campaigning on huge tax increases (but only for an evil few), and actually get votes! Lots of them. However, the amusing thing to me, is to see how these politically correct barons constantly lecture us on "paying our fair share," as if we're not, and all the while taking advantage of every trust and offshore account they can set up so that they, themselves aren't subject to these same tax burdens.

When you consider all the ways that we are taxed as citizens, it's a wonder that any politician can ever be reelected. It's a testament to our own insanity. After federal taxes, state taxes, county taxes, city taxes, sales taxes, gas taxes, hotel taxes, telephone taxes (looked at your phone bill lately?), estate taxes, use taxes, and government fees on everything from a fishing license to buying a car, it has been calculated that more than 60% of all the money you earn is demanded from you by law.

In biblical times the Jews were revolting over a 10% tax from Rome. It's a testament to the creative ways that our government extracts the money from us that we put up with it. We don't pay our taxes all at one time. No, we allow the government to take it from our paychecks, and then we hope that we can get some of it back at tax-time. It almost seems like some kind of bonus to us. If citizens had to sit down and write one check each year for their entire tax bill we'd suddenly have voter-imposed term limits.

But wait a minute, Larry. We're talking about Biblical precepts here. Aren't we supposed to take care of those less fortunate?

Yes, of course we are. There's no law that restricts us from helping those less fortunate if we want to. In fact, a later chapter will talk about the joys of doing just that. Remember also that we are commanded in the Bible to "render to Caesar." That means we are to pay our taxes and abide by the law. Some of these tax revenues do, in fact, go toward helping others less fortunate.

> **Matthew 22:21**
> "Render therefore unto Caesar the things which are Caesar's; and unto God the things that are God's." (NKJV)

Caesar has, however, inserted many things into the tax code (probably for Caesar's benefit!) that provide for legal ways to shelter certain income and reduce the tax burden. The problem is that the majority of the taxpayers in our country know very little about these tax strategies.

There is nothing morally wrong with taking advantage of existing laws to reduce your tax bill. Believe me, those with very large sums in their bank accounts know about these strategies.

In fact, I don't believe there is any reason why any family should leave any tax bill at death to their children, NO MATTER THE SIZE OF THE ESTATE. The one's who do have simply not educated themselves.

When it comes to taxes, there are 2 kinds: those you pay when you're alive, and those your estate pays for you after you die. Here's a few thoughts on both.

**Tax Reduction Today (while you're alive)**

So far we've been discussing how to achieve financial independence. In light of reaching the goal of being able to retire on your own terms, this section will show some immediate techniques in tax-reduction, and will be more applicable to achieving that goal.

What kind of things should you be doing to reduce those immediate taxes? Here's some good practices to fall into:

- **take maximum advantage of employer sponsored retirement plans.** Doing that will reduce your taxable income.

- **understand your tax situation.** When it comes to preparing your tax returns many folks leave everything to their CPA or tax-preparer. That's OK, but you should have a working knowledge of what you're paying and why. Once your brain starts percolating on those troubling line items you'll begin to adjust some behaviors to reduce that bottom line.

- **have you refinanced your home recently?** If so, don't overlook those points deductions that you are entitled to.

- **invest in dividend-paying stocks.** There is a more favorable tax rate on dividend income. This can make such investments more attractive than other cash generating securities, such as bonds.

- **Hold stocks for the long-term.** Just like dividends, long-term capital gains are taxed at a lower rate than ordinary income. By the way, long-term is defined as more than one year.

- **there can be deductions even for those who don't itemize**, such as student loan interest that you've paid, alimony, job-related moving expenses, etc. If you're self-employed take advantage of expenses and deduct when allowed. Keep track of everything.

- **you may be able to take advantage of certain credits** such as the Hope and Lifetime Learning credits, for students. There are also adoption credits and dependent-care credits you may be able to qualify for. The Earned Income Tax Credit will reduce your tax bill if you're a lower income earner.

- **if you're an unincorporated business owner** (and you can stomach it) **hire family members**. There can be significant tax benefits for doing this.

**Estate Tax Reduction (after you're dead)**

There are so many examples of the use of trusts and life insurance to reduce and eliminate estate taxes that it's impossible to reference all of them. Some of these techniques are complex (many financial advisors are ignorant of them), and a good estate tax attorney, knowledgable financial planner, and tax professional are all essential for structuring a good bulletproof plan.

Here's one example:  A Family Legacy Trust

This type of trust is intended for an extended period of time, usually multiple generations. Any funds put into this trust, if made irrevocable, are not countable in your estate after death. Also, creditors cannot touch it. Assuming the trust is initially funded with $500,000 and grows at 7% it could potentially be worth $7.5 million dollars after forty years, a very nice gift to your children and grandchildren. As trustee over the trust, your child (or children) will have control over the trust assets. It's possible to set the trust up in such a way that it will provide protection from lawsuits, divorce, and probate.

There are many different ways to protect your estate and children through the use of other trusts, such as Irrevocable Life Insurance Trusts, Revocable Living Trusts, and more. There is even an intentionally defective trust! All of these are designed to provide certain tax benefits, and can be constructed and combined in very special ways to allow you to pass your wealth to your descendants, and not to Uncle Sam!

If you have an estate of any size at all, the use of a trust of some kind is usually advisable. Talk to a knowledgable advisor about this.

## Chapter 10

# The Key to Happiness

If you were a young person starting out, and began to follow this "path to wealth" that I've laid out, using tried and true Biblical principles, you would inevitably find yourself well off financially after some working years had gone by.

Would you have had some bumps in the road? Of course! Everyone does. Perhaps you'd have had to change jobs, or had unexpected expenses. But no matter what, by following these methods you were able to handle everything that life threw at you. You have been a good steward of the resources that God gave you.

> **1 Timothy 6:17-19** "As for the rich in this present age, charge them not to be haughty, nor to set their hopes on the uncertainty of riches, but on God, who richly provides us with everything to enjoy. They are to do good, to be rich in good works, to be generous and ready to share, thus storing up treasure for themselves as a good foundation for the future, so that they may take hold of that which is truly life." (NRSV)

Now you have some things laid up for yourself. You are on track to reaching financial independence. Money, and where it will come from is not an overriding concern for you at this point. Now it's time to discover the real joy in life – helping those less fortunate than yourself.

You need to understand that all wealth comes from God, and the reason He gives us wealth is so that we can be generous with it. He cannot fill a tightly clinched fist.

*You will be made rich in every way so that you can be generous on every occasion, and through us your generosity will result in thanksgiving to God. (2 Corinthians 9:11)*

*One person gives freely, yet gains even more; another withholds unduly, but comes to poverty. (Proverbs 11:24)*

*Remember this: Whoever sows sparingly will also reap sparingly, and whoever sows generously will also reap generously. (2 Corinthians 9:6)*

You should be especially generous if you are well off!

*Command those who are rich ... to do good, to be rich in good deeds, and to be generous and willing to share. In this way they will lay up treasure for themselves as a firm foundation for the coming age, so that they may take hold of the life that is truly life. (1 Timothy 6:17-19)*

You can choose to believe all this or not, but it has been my observation that those who seem to do the best financially are the most generous (let's not count politicians….or those with hidden personal motives).

Let's face it, generosity makes our world a better place. Have you ever had someone help pick you up when you were down? Remember how good that felt? Studies have shown that generous people see the world differently. They are less stressed than most. They are generally optimistic. They have hope and bring it to others.

To be generous requires trust in others, and a certain amount of faith. They know that all of the problems of the world won't be solved by them, but they can help one person a great deal. As a general rule, generous people have bigger dreams than those who are stingy, and they realize that life is short. There is only a little time to leave our mark on it.

Generosity IS a legacy. A good one.

You will discover that there is a lot more than monetary gain for those that you help. You give them hope. You inspire them. Their world is truly brighter because you came into it. John Bunyon said that, "you have not lived until you have done something for someone who can never repay you." I believe that.

Being generous does something else for you. It will make you a grateful person. Before long your entire worldview will begin to change in a positive way. Now your money isn't just a tool to be held onto, but a path to freedom and happiness, by making others happy.

Who should you give to?

There are numerous charities and causes that will be happy to help you with your problem, and you'll get a tax deduction besides, but everyone has someone in their life that they can help. Just look around. With eyes looking to help others, you'll be surprised at what you'll see. Single mothers, those recently unemployed, even young people just starting out are great candidates for your generosity.

Be careful, though. Those with addictions and substance abuse problems will usually not reinforce your belief in the goodness of mankind. I'm afraid that our 21$^{st}$ century culture doesn't place the same value on hard work and honesty that it once did. There are some folks out there who have no shame, and ever live to take advantage of you. Use wisdom and discernment. There are organizations dedicated to helping the addicted, and they should be used as recipients for your generosity. Spare change, given on the street will likely be in the bar in a short time.

Being generous with your money, time, and other resources will bring you a great deal of enjoyment and satisfaction. Not only are you on the path to financial freedom, but you will be happy, and appreciated in the process.

And what's wrong with that?

## 11 Chapter

# Let's Make a Run for It!

If you're like me, you like short and succinct chapters when you read a book. Well, you're going to love this one!

There's just not a lot left to say. You have established your course and you have stuck to it. You have made wise investments and protected yourself against mayhem (you know….that bad guy on television). You are well known as a generous person.

The only thing left now is for you to grow that nest egg! Stick to the path, and get ready to smile as your financial picture begins to look better and better.

Who knows, you may even be one of the first of all your friends to retire.

## Chapter 12

# Touchdown!

Not long ago I was having a bite at a local fast-food joint. I noticed a lady who was probably on the high side of her seventies cleaning tables. It looked to me like this was maybe all she could physically do. While I applaud the firm that offered this lady a job, I couldn't help but reflect on why this woman was there.

I once interviewed a 65 year-old lady who told me that she received $714 a month from Social Security, still had a mortgage and two car payments. That was her only income. How does anyone get by on that amount of money in 2016? A lifetime of bad financial choices had taken it's toll. That was probably the case with the fast-food lady too.

When I began to conceive the idea of this book I was well aware that many of the biggest names in finance had already written books. Those books are very well done.

So why write another one?

It was because I discovered that the vast majority of them were written for sophisticated people who already had resources. These books could tell you how to set up an Irrevocable Life Insurance Trust. They could explain the best tax havens where you could move your money offshore. They could show you the benefits of setting up an Intentionally Defective Grantors Trust.

But there was not much out there to help the little guy become financially successful and satisfied. Throw in writing about Biblical principles that cannot fail, and there's almost nothing. That's why I wrote this book.

My intention here is to offer a short, readable, and easily followed path to success. It will work every time, if you follow it for a lifetime.

What if you don't have a lifetime? What if you're in your fifties, or even retired? Then it's time to get started now, wherever you happen to be in life. Of course, the longer the timeframe that you have the better, but it's never too late to get started.

So that's it. Set yourself up for financial success. Make a plan, don't procrastinate, and get going, then teach your children how to do the same. They'll be forever grateful.

Larry Jones is the owner of NavStar Financial Services located in the Lake Norman area of North Carolina. He has been awarded the Chartered Financial Consultant designation by the American College in Bry Mawr, Pennsylvania. He's also an investment advisor representative with Horter Financial Management, LLC located in Cincinnati, Ohio.

When not working he enjoys golf, any form of boating, playing guitar, and reading. He's also a member of the Gideons, is active in his church, and other community organizations.

Married to the greatest woman on earth, Sherry and still very close with his Son, Adam, he will be the first to say that over twenty years of walking with Christ hasn't done him any harm. He considers himself very, very blessed.

You can e-mail him at larry@navfs.com  (www.navfs.com)

www.ingramcontent.com/pod-product-compliance
Lightning Source LLC
Chambersburg PA
CBHW070313230526
45470CB00002B/854